IGNITING WRITING

1

Pie Corbett • Sue Palmer • Ann Webley

Nelson Thornes

Published in 2006 by:
Nelson Thornes Ltd
Delta Place
27 Bath Road
CHELTENHAM
GL53 7TH
United Kingdom

12 / 10 9 8 7 6 5 4

A catalogue record for this book is available from the British Library

ISBN 978 0 7487 9729 5

Illustrations by Tom Bamfield and Can Studios.
Page make-up by Pantek Arts, Maidstone, Kent

Printed in China by 1010 Printing International Ltd

Contents

Introduction

When you are working on your own, this book will help you to:

- think about what to include
- plan your work and make notes
- decide how to organise your writing in sections or paragraphs
- choose the right sorts of words and sentences for the kind of writing you are doing
- edit and improve your work when you have finished.

The *Igniting Writing* whiteboard sequences will help you learn about writing. Examples of these are given for each unit.

Contents of the CDs

CD 1: Journeys	
Sequence	**Text type**
Theme: Quests	
Story of a Quest	Story
Dispatches from a Quest	Letter writing
Scenes from a Quest	Playscript
Theme: Jets	
The Jet Engine	Explanation
Air Safety	Instructions
Jet Travel: Good or Bad?	Persuasion (L) Discussion (U)
Theme: Pilgrimages	
The Annual Hajj	Diary
Hindu Pilgrimages	Poetry
A Visit to Jerusalem	Recount
Theme: Space Travel	
Guide to the Planet Marco	Report
Outer Space, Outer Mind	Website/Advert
Finding Blue	Science fiction story

CD 2: Waterworlds	
Sequence	**Text type**
Theme: Titanic	
The Biggest and Best	Information text
The Sinking of the Titanic	Newspaper report
Water, Ice and Reflections	Poetry
Theme: Shipwreck!	
Diary of a Cabin Boy	Diary
Shipwreck!	Narrative
Water Cycle	Explanation (U)
Theme: Atlantis	
Atlantis – a Perfect World	Brochure
The Search for Atlantis	Story
Atlantis Found!	Playscript
Theme: Creatures of the Deep	
The Great White Shark	Report
Dolphins – Our Best Friend?	Persuasion
Does the Loch Ness Monster Exist?	Discussion

Writing stories

How do good writers create stories that keep you reading right until the very end? Some of the ingredients that make up a good story are covered in this book. However, when you are writing a story, it is important to think about mixing the ingredients together.

Look at the extract below:

> Nat trudged wearily down to the hen house. 'I don't need help,' he muttered, as he pushed past the dozing dwarf. Thog glanced up and wondered what was wrong with his old friend ...

Key: *character* · setting · plot

Can you see how information about the characters, setting and plot is mixed together? When you are writing your own stories, make sure you think carefully about how you can blend the different story aspects.

Even the very best writers spend time editing their stories, so that they are as enjoyable for the reader as possible. Go back to your stories after you have written them. How can they be even better than they already are? Try reading your story aloud, to hear how it sounds. And finally, remember that practice makes perfect: the more you write, the better you'll become!

Characters

Getting ideas

Think of someone that you know, have seen or met. Write down a description of them, and then change a few details. You can also use pictures from books and magazines.

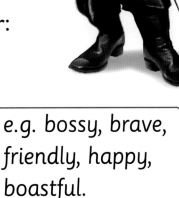

1. Decide on a name, e.g. Fantastic Mr Felix.

2. Think of a few details about your character:
    *   wears boots and a hat.
    *   a magical cat who can talk.

3. Decide how your character is feeling.

> e.g. bossy, brave, friendly, happy, boastful.

Building your character

*   How do others react to your character, e.g. *they are amazed, frightened, pleased.*

*   What do others say about him, e.g. *'Felix is so boastful,'* said Princess Petunia.

*   Show how the story changes the character.

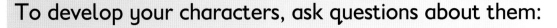

WRITER'S TOOLKIT

To develop your characters, ask questions about them:

✔ How old are they?

✔ What are they interested in?

✔ Do they have anything they really dislike?

✔ Have they a special talent?

LANGUAGE TOOLKIT

What do your characters look like?

✔ Choose one or two **details**, e.g. Felix wore long, black boots, a velvet cloak and a bright red top hat.

Show how they feel through what they say.

✔ Use powerful **speech verbs**, e.g. 'Oooh, my favourite! A saucer of cream,' he <u>purred</u>.

Show how they feel by what they do.

✔ Use powerful **verbs**, e.g. He <u>leapt</u> onto the broomstick.

Settings

1. ## What sort of story are you going to write?

   Look at the table on page 23. Use a setting that fits the type of story you are going to write.

2. ## Use a place that you know

   Set your story in a place that you know, e.g. your school, your home or on holiday.

3. ## Picture it

   Find a picture that fits with the story you would like to write. Imagine that you have to describe the picture to someone who cannot see it.

   This picture could be the setting for a story that takes place at home.

4. ## Close your eyes

   Imagine that you are standing in the picture:
   - **What can you hear?**

     Simon listened closely. He heard it again. It was a faint scrabble. It was definitely coming from the wardrobe.
   - **What can you feel?**

     Simon opened the wardrobe door and stepped inside. He pushed his way past old coats that brushed against his face.
   - **What can you smell?**

     He breathed in the musty smell of old clothes.

WRITER'S TOOLKIT

✔ Think of places you know and use your imagination.

✔ For different settings, use details so that the reader can 'see' the setting for themselves.

✔ Show the setting through the main character's eyes.

  As Simon's eyes got used to the dim light inside the wardrobe, he saw a small door.

✔ Choose an interesting name for your setting.

✔ Think about the time of day and the weather.

✔ Set the scene at the opening.

  Toys and books were scattered over his bedroom floor.

✔ Set the scene at the ending.

  He had never thought he would be so pleased to see his own bedroom again!

Fiction

LANGUAGE TOOLKIT

Have you used:

✔ a **list** to build a picture, e.g.

> blue curtains, red carpet and a blazing fire

✔ **adjectives** to describe, e.g.

> musty old coats

✔ **similes?** e.g.

> the old coats, like ghosts from another life

Creating plots

Getting ideas

A good storywriter is always on the lookout for a story idea. You need a story built around a 'problem'. You might get ideas from:

- stories that you have read

- retelling or changing traditional tales, nursery rhymes or story poems

- things that happen to you.

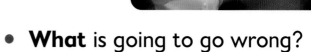

Start by mixing together your ingredients:

- **Who** is the main character?
- **Where** is he/she?
- **What** is he/she doing?
- **What** is going to go wrong?
- **How** will it end?

Story patterns

What kind of story are you writing? Look at page 23 to see a list of different types of stories. Here are some ideas:

- school/home problems
- going on a journey (or quest) to find something or to give something back
- conquer the monster
- finding a magical object that allows you to go on adventures
- traditional tales or a fairy story plot (*'Once upon a time …'*).

How to plan

Before you start to write your story, it is important to plan what will happen. Think about what will happen next, but keep the plot simple and clear. Here are some useful planning tools for different types of stories.

Flowcharts

A flowchart is ideal for planning a play or a story that takes place in different settings.

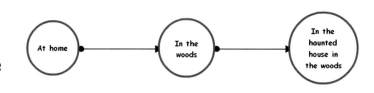

Timelines

A timeline is helpful for planning a letter or a diary. It allows you to put events in the right order.

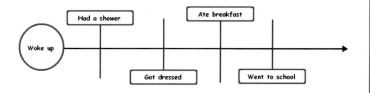

Storyboards

A storyboard is a good way of planning if you like to see how each scene will look.

Story picture maps

You might find a story picture map useful if you are writing a quest.

Story mountain

A story mountain is a good way of making sure that your plot is based around a problem or difficulty that the characters have to solve.

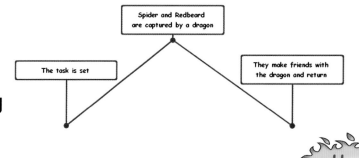

WRITER'S TOOLKIT

Have you:

✔ used your plan to help you write your story

✔ controlled the dialogue, or is there too much

✔ developed each part of the story properly

✔ written an ending that shows how the main character feels or what has been learned?

LANGUAGE TOOLKIT

Have you:

✔ stayed in the same **tense**

✔ stayed in the same **person**, e.g. *I* or *he/she*

✔ used words to link ideas, sentences and make paragraph changes?

Well-known stories can be rewritten by changing them, e.g. rewriting *Little Red Riding Hood* in a modern setting and making it about a boy visiting his gran's and being chased by a bully.

Writing dialogue

WRITER'S TOOLKIT

✔ Think about who is speaking and how they are feeling, e.g. 'Please don't take me away,' begged Matt.

✔ Think about the sort of thing the character would say.

✔ Use the dialogue to move the action forwards, e.g. 'Take us to the Ice Castle!' commanded the Ice Queen.

✔ Listen to the sorts of things people say and steal ideas!

✔ Try to break up the speech by writing about what the characters are doing, e.g. 'Take us to the Ice Castle!' commanded the Ice Queen. She gathered up the reins and tightened her grip on Matt, as the swan prepared to take off.

LANGUAGE TOOLKIT

✔ Put what is said inside **speech marks**.

✔ Put any **punctuation** inside the speech marks, e.g.
'Please don't take me away,' begged Matt.
'Take us to the Ice Castle!' commanded the Ice Queen.
'Where are you taking me?' asked Matt.

✔ Start a **new line** whenever a new speaker speaks.

Using paragraphs

Why do we need paragraphs?

Paragraphs help writers to organise their thoughts or ideas. They also make it easier for the reader to follow the storyline.

How to write in paragraphs

Try building paragraphs into your plan. Do this by using boxes in a flowchart or a story mountain, where you make each 'part' of the story into a paragraph.

Look at the example below from 'Scenes from a Quest'.

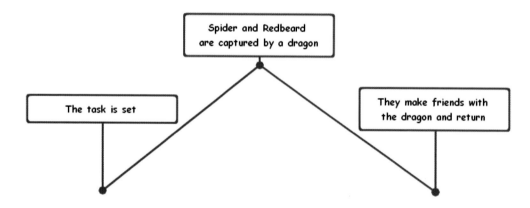

When to change paragraphs

Remember to change paragraphs when you change each part of the story. It is also important to remember to start a new line whenever you have a new person speaking:

'Hi,' said Tim.
'Good morning,' muttered Bill.

WRITER'S TOOLKIT

The main types of paragraph are:

✔ **opening** – set the scene, introduce the main character

✔ **build-up** – get the story going; your character is doing something

✔ **problem** – something goes wrong

✔ **problem solved** – everything is ok

✔ **ending** – show what has been learned or how your character has changed.

LANGUAGE TOOLKIT

Have you used:

✔ connectives to open paragraphs, e.g. ⟨ Later that day

✔ short openings, e.g. ⟨ They ran!

✔ character openings, e.g. ⟨ Bill frowned.

✔ words to link ideas within paragraphs? e.g. ⟨ and, so, as, but, because, while, when

Style

Style is the word we use to describe the way in which a story is told.

Developing your writing style

Good writing style means:

- choosing good words
- varying your sentences.

Remember to link the story together by making sure you stay in the same tense.

Choosing good words

It is worth keeping a writing journal and collecting words to use. Notice well-chosen words when you are reading and store them away.

Varying your sentences

Invent and build up a store of different types of sentences. Jot these in your writing journal. Notice how good writers vary their sentences. Try copying different sentence patterns:

- **Short**: *He stared at the poodle.*
- **Long**: *They watched as the enormous dragon dragged itself across the glittering pile of treasure and burped.*
- **Questions**: (to make the reader wonder) *Would they find it?*
- **Exclamations**: (for impact) *Run for it!*
- **'When' sentences**: *The next day it rained …*
- **'How' sentences**: *Sadly, he knelt down …*
- **'Where' sentences**: *In a distant valley …*
- **Sentence of three for description**: (to build up a picture) *He stared at the piles of pearls, glittering coins and precious metals.*

- **Sentence of three for action**: (to speed up action) *The dragon grinned, opened its jaws and hissed.*

WRITER'S TOOLKIT

Try to vary the **openings** to sentences:

✔ How? – *Calmly, she walked on …*

✔ Where? – *Under the hill was a mine …*

✔ When? – *After that, they went home …*

LANGUAGE TOOLKIT

Have you used:

✔ precise **nouns**, e.g. — Alsatian **not** dog

✔ well-chosen **adjectives**, e.g. — shy giant **not** big giant

✔ powerful **verbs**, e.g. — staggered **not** went

✔ **similes**, e.g. — like a giant

✔ **alliteration**? e.g. — the dragon drank

Here is an example of some writing taken from a quest story. Look at how the writer has varied the sentences.

At that moment the Wizard banged his wooden stick on the floor. The kitchen door flew open. There stood Spider's companion, Redbeard. He was a small and rather fierce-looking dwarf who was dressed in a scarlet cloak.

17

Poetry

Gather your ideas

First of all, you need to decide what you are going to write about:

1. Look closely at the world around you. Look at your subject as if you are seeing it for the first time. What does it remind you of? Jot down your ideas in a notebook.

2. You could also start by studying a photograph or picture. Label the picture. Use the writer's toolkit to make your labels as interesting as possible.

3. Another starting point for a poem can be something that has happened to you. What could you see/hear/taste/smell/touch as you lived through the experience? Make it come alive for your reader.

4. Sometimes ideas come to you when you least expect them! Why don't you keep a poetry notebook? In it, you could write down:

   - ideas or notes

   - a word store of interesting words you might be able to use

   - other people's poems that you think are interesting.

Organise your ideas

Now you can organise your ideas into a form. Look at the table of different types of poems on page 23.

WRITER'S TOOLKIT

✔ Create pictures in your poems by using similes, e.g.

> The moon shone like a pale mirror

✔ Create sounds in your poems by using alliteration, e.g.

> a kind cow crept by

LANGUAGE TOOLKIT

Have you used:

✔ powerful **verbs**, e.g. — snapped **not** said

✔ well-chosen **adjectives**, e.g. — rusty letter box **not** red letter box

✔ **playful** word combinations, e.g. — buttery sunlight

✔ **repetition** for effect?

Playscripts

Where to start?

A play is a story that is performed by actors. You could begin by taking a story that you know well and turning it into a play. Another way of writing a play is to make it up as you act it out with a friend. Then you can write it down.

What sort of play do you want to put on?

Think about how much time you have. Where are you going to perform it? Who is going to come to your play?

Then decide on the type of performance you want:

- play
- video
- radio drama
- puppet show.

Ask yourself if you need:

- scenery
- costumes
- lighting
- props
- make-up
- sound effects.

During the play

When the play is being performed your actors will need to remember:

- to speak clearly
- to use plenty of expression
- to be loud enough
- to keep in their 'role'.

WRITER'S TOOLKIT

✔ List the characters at the start of the play.

✔ Organise the play into scenes.

✔ Put the name of the speaker on the left.

✔ Put stage directions in italics/brackets to show what characters should do, if it is not obvious but is important.

LANGUAGE TOOLKIT

✔ Do not use **speech marks** or **speech verbs**.

✔ Write your play like a **conversation**.

✔ Make sure what the actors say suggests how they feel.

✔ Speech may use:

- contracted forms (don't)

- everyday expressions (don't give me grief).

This is a scene from a play. Can you see how the writer has used the checklists above?

The scene is set in a small kitchen with a table in the centre. There is a wooden bench behind the table plus a chair for visitors. To the left there is a side table with pots, pans, plates, knives and forks, a kettle and mugs. On the opposite side of the stage there is a small cooker.

Spider stares at the old Wizard as he enters and sits down.

Wizard: Do not look afraid, young Spider.

Spider (*nervously*): Would you like a cup of acorn tea?

Spider gets tea and a plate of bread.

Wizard: Now, that is a better welcome.

Spider: Wwwwwhat would you like?

Creating suspense

To make your writing really exciting, try to build up suspense. This means letting the reader begin to think that something bad might happen. Some ideas are given below.

1. In your story, put your character into a situation where everything is going well. Show them doing something they enjoy:

   Kiri wandered back into the classroom. She sat down at her table and began to cut out the different pictures from the magazine. Mrs Jennings would be pleased with her.

2. Then introduce some suspense by letting your character hear or see something unusual. This warns the reader that something scary is about to happen, e.g. *she heard a moan.*

3. When you are writing a suspense paragraph, try to see what is happening in your mind. It helps if you make the scene dark and cold. It also helps if the character is alone. Try to show how the main character reacts, e.g. *she began to shake.*

   At that moment, Kiri heard footsteps in the corridor. Somebody was walking down to the classroom. Who was it? Nervously, Kiri glanced up. She was just in time to see a dark shadow at the door. At that moment, the lights went out. Kiri screamed.

WRITER'S TOOLKIT

✔ Use short sentences, e.g. Kiri glanced up.
✔ Use powerful verbs, e.g. glanced.
✔ Introduce a glimpse, e.g. a dark shadow.
✔ Introduce a sound effect, e.g. footsteps.
✔ Use a question to make the reader wonder, e.g. who was it?

Story/poetry types

Story type	Characters	Settings	Key features
Adventure	Hero; heroine; baddy	Island; cave; tunnel	Cliff hangers; action
School/Home	Teacher; friends; gangs; bully	Playground; classroom; journey to school	Everyday events can be used as a plot
Traditional	Princess; king; ogre; magical creatures	Forest; palace; tower; market; cave	Good vs evil; events in threes
Myths	Animals; people; gods; elements (moon, stars, mountains, etc.)	Countries all round the world; different cultures	Stories explain how or why things happen
Legends	Real people from history, e.g. Robin Hood	Village; town; city; forest	Past tense based on real events but exaggerated
Fables	Animals instead of people	Forest; village	A weakness (greed, etc.) leads to a downfall; moral at end

Poem type	Features
Tongue twisters	Repeated sounds that are hard to say, e.g. *She sells sea shells on the sea shore*
Riddles	Guessing poem; often using similes/metaphors
Nonsense	Invented words, e.g. *squirtle*; fantastical ideas; often rhyming, e.g. *Twas brillig and the slithy toves did gyre and gimble in the wabe*
Lists	Repeated pattern or phrase, e.g. *last night I saw the moon singing, last night I saw the stars dancing*
Alphabet	Alphabet letters used to list ideas, e.g. *a is an ant that ate an apple, b is a beetle that bought a banana*
Counting	Numbers used to list ideas, e.g. *1 old Oxford ox, 2 tired tiny turtles*
Observation	Based on looking carefully; using adjectives, similes, metaphors to describe
Shape	Poem written in the shape of the subject

Non-fiction writing

There are lots of different kinds of non-fiction texts. In this book you will find **toolkits** to help you remember how to write non-fiction.

Whenever you write non-fiction, remember to:

- write an **opening**
- organise different parts of your writing into **sections** or **paragraphs**
- use **topic words** (words to do with the subject you are writing about)
- use **clear descriptions** (choose adjectives or adverbs that help make the information easy to understand or interesting)
- use **connectives**
- write an **ending**.

You can use the toolkits whenever you are writing, for example, literacy, history, geography or science.

Planning and making notes

You can use the **skeleton diagrams** in this book to help you plan and make notes.

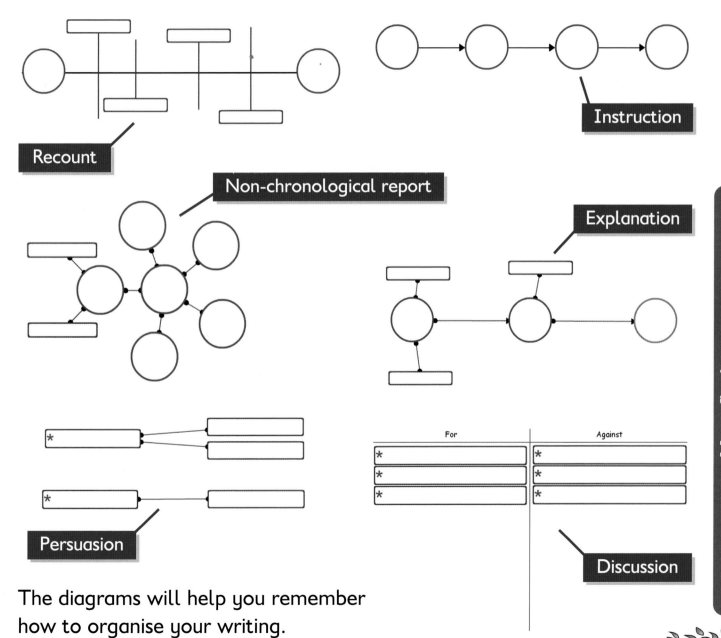

Recount

Instruction

Non-chronological report

Explanation

Persuasion

For		Against	
*		*	
*		*	
*		*	

Discussion

The diagrams will help you remember how to organise your writing.

When writing notes remember to:

- Read through the information so that you understand it. You might have to read information in more than one place so be careful not to repeat your notes.

- Note down the main points that you want to write about in **key words** or **pictures**.

- Add **more words** and **simple phrases** on the other lines on the diagram to show the facts or examples that you plan to write about. These are memory joggers so you can remember to write about them in detail. **Do not write sentences**. You can see how this is done in this example of the start of a plan of a report from 'The Great White Shark'.

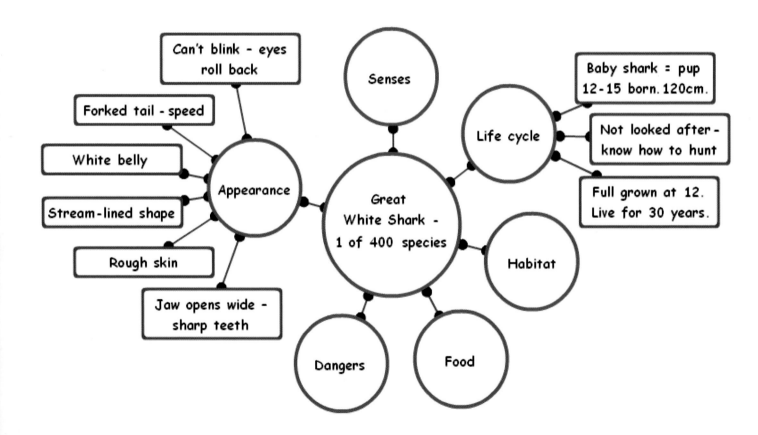

- Plan an **opening** and an **ending**.

- Think about whether you want to add anything to your writing such as:

  - diagrams

  - pictures with captions

  - charts

  - sub-headings.

Now you are ready to write!

You can use the pages in this book to help you remember what to do.

Make sure you think about **what the writing is for** and **who is going to read it**.

Your writing needs to be **interesting** and **full of detail**.

Writing recounts

<table>
<tr><td>

What is it for?

A recount tells us about something that has happened.

</td><td>

+

</td><td>

Who is it for?

It is for someone who wants to know all about what has happened.

</td></tr>
</table>

There are lots of different kinds of **recount**. For example:

- a write-up of a trip or activity

- an account of something that happened in history

- a letter to tell someone about an event

- a diary

- a newspaper article about something that happened.

Look at the example below from 'Diary of a Cabin Boy'.

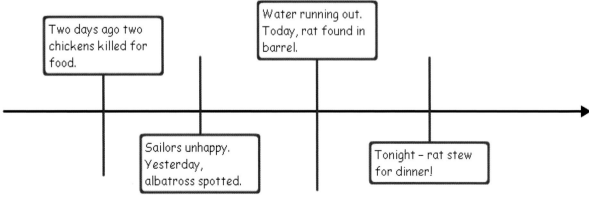

Two days ago two chickens killed for food.

Water running out. Today, rat found in barrel.

Sailors unhappy. Yesterday, albatross spotted.

Tonight – rat stew for dinner!

Organisation toolkit

Remember to:

- write a **title** to say what you are writing about

- write an **opening** that sets the scene. You could try to answer the questions who?, what?, where?, when? and why?

- write about events in **time order**. Put the events in different sections or paragraphs

- write an **ending**. This could say how you (or someone else) felt about what happened.

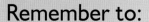

LANGUAGE TOOLKIT

Remember to:

✔ write in the **past tense**

✔ use **time connectives** (next, after that, in the morning)

✔ include the **names of people** and **places** (Sancto, King Henry VIIth)

✔ use other **topic words** (ropes and pulleys, turn the sails)

✔ use **clear descriptions** (travelling into the wildest oceans)

✔ pick out details that will be **interesting** to the reader.

Non-fiction

Writing non-chronological reports

What is it for?

A report gives information. It tells us what places or things are like.

+

Who is it for?

It is for someone who wants to know about something.

There are lots of different kinds of **report**. For example:

- an information leaflet
- a newspaper article
- a letter
- a non-fiction book, e.g. information about the Roman army in a history book
- a school website.

Look at this example from 'Guide to Planet Marco'.

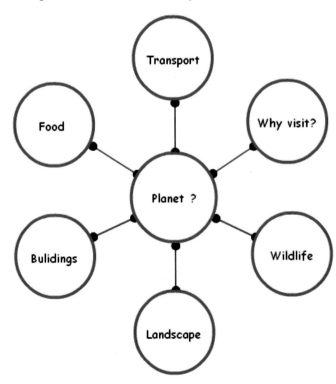

Organisation toolkit

Remember to:

- write a **title** that interests the reader, e.g., *The Great White Shark – Killer of the Seas*
- write an **opening** sentence that says what you are writing about
- write your information in different **paragraphs**. You could give each one a **sub-heading** to say what it is about
- put your paragraphs in an order
- draw **pictures** or **diagrams** if they help to give the information more clearly
- write an **ending** sentence. You could try to say how interesting you find the subject.

LANGUAGE TOOLKIT

Remember to:

✔ write in the **present tense**, unless you are writing a report about something in the past

✔ write in the **third person** (he, she, it, they)

✔ use **topic words** (teleportation, space pod)

✔ use **clear descriptions** (towers made of a hard see-through crystal)

✔ include **interesting** detail so that your reader enjoys the report, e.g. (Marconians like to end their meals by chewing twigs from the Calashom tree).

Writing instructions

<table>
<tr>
<td>

What is it for?

Instructions tell us how to do or make something.

</td>
<td>

+

</td>
<td>

Who is it for?

Instructions are for someone who needs to know how to do or make something.

</td>
</tr>
</table>

There are lots of different kinds of **instructions**. For example:

- a recipe
- an instruction poster, e.g. on how to use a computer
- notices around your school
- an instruction leaflet, e.g. how to make a hand puppet or safety instructions on an aeroplane.

Look at the example below from 'Air Safety'.

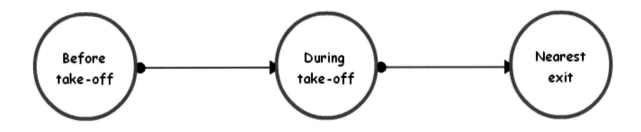

Organisation toolkit

Remember to:

- write a **title** to say what you are writing about, e.g. What to do in an emergency

- write an **opening** sentence that makes the reader want to follow the instructions, e.g. Follow these instructions and you'll always be safe

- write a list of '**what you need**' before you start, if necessary

- write a list of **what to do** in the **order** they must be done. You can **number** each line if you want to

- draw **pictures** or **diagrams** if they help to give the information more clearly

- write an **ending** sentence, e.g. Now you can settle back and enjoy the ride.

LANGUAGE TOOLKIT

Remember to:

✔ use **bossy verbs** (<u>pull</u> the strap to tighten the belt)

✔ use **time connectives** (first, next)

✔ use **topic words** (buckle, seatbelt, aisle, luggage)

✔ use **clear descriptions**. Try to choose words to help the reader follow your instructions (store <u>small</u> items under seats, walk, <u>quickly</u> to the nearest exit).

Writing explanations

What is it for?

An explanation states **how** or **why** something happens, or **how** something works

+

Who is it for?

It is for someone who wants to understand something.

There are lots of different kinds of **explanations**. For example:

- a question and answer leaflet
- a letter
- a non-fiction book
- an encyclopaedia entry.

Look at the example below from 'The Jet Engine'.

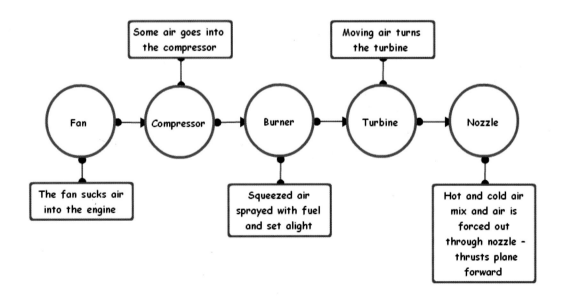

Organisation toolkit

Remember to:

- write a **title** to say what you are writing about
- write your information in **the order that things happen**
- draw a **diagram** if it helps make your explanation clearer
- use **bullet points** or **sub-headings** if this helps break up the explanation.

LANGUAGE TOOLKIT

Remember to:

- ✔ write in the **present tense**, unless you are writing an explanation about something in the past
- ✔ write in the **third person** (it, they)
- ✔ use **time connectives** to show the order clearly (first, next, then)
- ✔ use words to show **how** or **why** (because, so, this means that)
- ✔ use **topic words** (engine, fan, blades, fuel)
- ✔ use **clear descriptions** (The <u>hot</u> air then joins up with the <u>cooler</u> air).

Non-fiction

Writing persuasion

What is it for?

Persuasive writing is for putting across your own point of view about something to try to make people agree with it.

+

Who is it for?

It is for anyone who might be interested in the subject, but might have a very different point of view. This means you have to include lots of facts and lots of reasons to try to make them agree with you.

There are lots of different kinds of **persuasive writing**. For example:

- an advertisement
- a poster or flier
- a book 'blurb'
- a newspaper or magazine article

- a leaflet, e.g. from people who want to stop whale hunting
- a letter, e.g. from someone trying to persuade somebody to do something.

Look at the example opposite from 'Dolphins'.

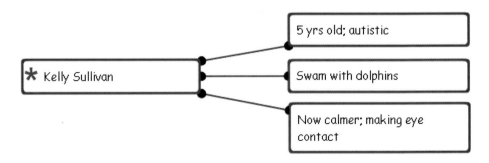

* Kelly Sullivan

- 5 yrs old; autistic
- Swam with dolphins
- Now calmer; making eye contact

Organisation toolkit

Remember to:

- write an **eye-catching title** to say what you are writing about

- write an **opening** which states your point of view

- write your points in different sections or **paragraphs**. Start each one with a **topic sentence** that says what you think

- use **bullet points**, **sub-headings** and **pictures** if these help to make your points clearer

- write an **ending** that re-states your point of view.

LANGUAGE TOOLKIT

Remember to:

✔ write in the **present tense**

✔ choose **powerful verbs** and **strong adjectives** and **adverbs** to help give your point of view (*I think this is* <u>*dreadfully cruel*</u> *because dolphins are* <u>*trapped*</u>)

✔ use words to give **reasons** for your point of view (*because, so, this means that*)

✔ use **topic words** (*tuna, nets, swim*)

✔ use **connecting phrases** to signal your points (*first of all, also*).

Writing discussion

What is it for?

A discussion puts forward both sides of an argument. It gives points **for** and **against**.

+

Who is it for?

It is for anyone who is interested in the subject. They might be trying to make up their mind by reading what you have written.

There are lots of different kinds of **discussion writing**. For example:

- a leaflet about both sides of an issue

- a newspaper article

- information in non-fiction books.

Look at this example from 'Loch Ness'.

Does the Loch Ness monster exist?	
For (Nicky)	Against (Adam)
✶ Sightings & photos	✶ Sightings & photos
✶ Expedition	✶ No scientific proof
✶ Don't have to see to believe	✶ Conditions in loch

Organisation toolkit

Remember to:

- write a **title** to say what you are writing about

- write an **opening** that states what the discussion is about

- write your points **for** and **against** in different sections or **paragraphs**. Start each one with a **topic sentence** that shows which side you are writing about

- use **sub-headings** if this helps to make your points clearer

- write an **ending** that says what you think.

LANGUAGE TOOLKIT

Remember to:

✔ write in the **present tense**, unless you are writing a discussion about something in the past

✔ write mainly in the **third person** (it, he, they)

✔ use **topic words** (humps, lake creature)

✔ use words to show **reasons** (because, so)

✔ use **descriptions** to help make the facts clear (<u>deep</u> caves, <u>two</u> humps)

✔ use words to signal **both sides** of the argument (Some people say ... Other people think ...)

✔ use **connecting phrases** to signal your points (first of all, also)

✔ use **examples** to back up what you say.

Writing letters

What is it for?

There are lots of reasons for writing a letter. For example, to send news and keep in touch, to thank someone, to complain or to invite someone or something.

+

Who is it for?

A letter could be for a friend or relation (a **personal** letter) or someone you don't know (a **formal** letter).

Look at the examples below of a personal letter and a formal letter from 'Dispatches from a Quest'.

Personal letter

Dear Bramble,

Thog and I have been travelling for so long that we can hardly remember what home looks like any more.
First we had to cross the great mountains. There we got caught in a blizzard. It was so cold that I thought we would not survive.

Look after my hens and whatever happens, do not let anyone else steal my old tinder box.

Your friend - Nat the hen keeper

Formal letter

Dear Sir,

I am writing to complain about the items that I bought from your shop last moon-month.

I will be calling at your shop once this adventure is over and expect a refund for these goods.

Yours faithfully,
Nat Treegood

Organisation toolkit for a personal letter

Remember to:

- write **your address** in the **top right** hand part of the page
- write the **date** underneath the address
- start your letter on the **left** hand side of the paper
- explain why you are writing in the **first sentence**
- set out your letter in **paragraphs**. Start each one on a new line with a **topic sentence**
- **sign off** your letter on a new line
- make your letter **detailed** and **interesting**.

Organisation toolkit for a formal letter

Remember to:

- write **your address** in the **top right** hand part of the page
- write the **date** underneath the address
- write the address of the person the letter is for. Write this lower down than the date and on the **left** hand side of the page
- start your letter **underneath** the other person's address
- explain why you are writing in the **first sentence**
- set out your letter in **paragraphs**. Start each one on a new line with a **topic sentence**
- **sign off** your letter on a new line
- make your letter **clear** and **detailed**.

Writing diaries

What is it for?

A diary or journal records what happens in your life. You can also write about your thoughts and feelings. Sometimes people like to read their diaries in the future to help them remember things that happened.

+

Who is it for?

A diary or journal is for the writer of the diary.

Look at the example below from 'The Annual Hajj'.

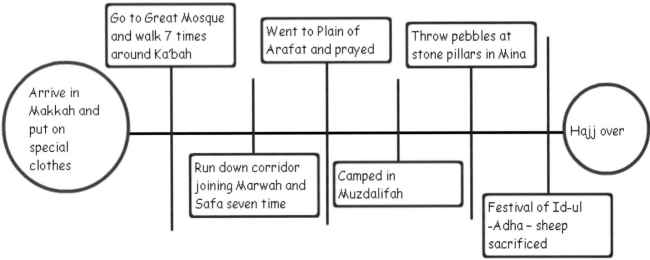

Go to Great Mosque and walk 7 times around Ka'bah

Went to Plain of Arafat and prayed

Throw pebbles at stone pillars in Mina

Arrive in Makkah and put on special clothes

Run down corridor joining Marwah and Safa seven time

Camped in Muzdalifah

Hajj over

Festival of Id-ul -Adha – sheep sacrificed

A diary is a special kind of **recount**.

Look at the toolkits on page 29.

You need to include these features and also look at the toolkits below.

Organisation toolkit

Remember to:

• write the **date** at the start of the diary entry.

LANGUAGE TOOLKIT

Remember to:

✔ write about what happened in the **past tense**

✔ include details about your feelings. You can write these in the **present tense** (How fantastic, I hope I get one! I can take it into school when I get home.)

✔ use a **chatty style**, as though you are talking to your diary (Imagine – every Muslim in the world turns towards Mecca five times a day to pray.)

✔ write lots of **interesting detail**. (It is called the 'Kiswa'. It gets cut up at the end of the Hajj so people can take home a small piece as a reminder.)

Writing newspaper articles

There are lots of different kinds of articles in newspapers but the most common is the **news story**.

What is it for?

A news story tells people what has been happening.

+

Who is it for?

It is for the readers of the newspaper who are interested to find out the news.

There are lots of different kinds of newspapers and magazines, for example:

- a local newspaper, for people who live in a certain area
- a school newspaper, for everyone connected with the school
- magazines about different topics: computer games, model-making, music, cooking, gardening. These are for people who like these activities
- comics, usually for children.

Newspapers and magazines contain:

- news stories
- interviews
- letters
- advertisements
- puzzles
- reports.

A news story in a newspaper is a special kind of **recount**.

Look at the toolkits on page 29.

You need to include those features and also look at the toolkits below.

Look at the example below from 'The Sinking of the Titanic'.

> **THE DAILY TIMES**
> April 17th 1912
>
> **TITANIC HAS SUNK!**
> At 11.40pm on April 14th, the world's largest ocean liner skimmed the side of an iceberg in the Atlantic Ocean. Three hours later she had sunk. Over 1500 people have drowned or been frozen to death in the icy waters.

Organisation toolkit

Remember to:

- give your paper a **name** if you are writing a front page. Add the **date**
- write an exciting **headline** (Titanic was sunk!)
- write an **opening** that says what the story is about (who? what? where? when? why?)
- write your story in **columns**
- divide your information into **sections**. Use **sub-headings**
- include **pictures with captions**
- write an **ending**.

LANGUAGE TOOLKIT

Remember to:

✔ write your story in a way that will interest the reader

✔ use **powerful verbs** and **adjectives**.

Writing alphabetical reference texts

What is it for?

A reference text helps people find out what they want to know.

+

Who is it for?

It is for someone who wants to find out something as quickly as possible.

There are many different kinds of **alphabetical reference texts**. For example:

- a **dictionary** gives the meaning of words
- a **spelling dictionary** helps with the spelling of words
- a **rhyming dictionary** lists words that rhyme
- a **thesaurus** shows words that have the same meaning
- an **encyclopaedia** contains the main facts about many topics
- an **index** helps to find information in a book
- a **glossary** gives the meaning of special words to do with the subject.

These can all be **digital** texts on the computer. You might find these useful when you write stories, poems and non-fiction.

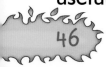

Organisation toolkit

Remember to:

- give the page a **heading**
- use other **headings** to help the reader
- sort out the **key words** in **alphabetical order**
- write the key words in **bold print** to make them stand out
- use a **layout** that makes it easy for the reader to find what they want
- add **pictures** or **diagrams** if they help the reader.

LANGUAGE TOOLKIT

Remember to:

✔ decide if you are going to write in **notes** or **sentences**

✔ write in the **third** person in sentences

✔ use **clear**, **simple** language.

Editing writing

1. Think about the **writing task**.

   - What sort of writing is it?

   - Who is it for?

   - Have you done what you were asked to do?

   - Will your reader understand it?

   - Have you organised your work clearly?

   - Have you included enough detail?

   - Is your writing interesting?

2. Look at ways to **improve your sentences**, for example:

   - make words count by changing weak verbs or adjectives

   - make sure that you start sentences in different ways

   - check that you have found different ways of connecting your sentences and ideas.

3. Check your **spelling** and **punctuation**. (It is often easier to spot mistakes if you read your work aloud.)